AF575649

Library of Congress Control Number: 2019947427

Designed by Justin Watkinson
Technical Layout by Jack Chappell
Type set in Impact/Minion Pro/Univers LT Std

ISBN: 978-0-7643-5940-8
Printed in China

Published by Schiffer Publishing, Ltd.
4880 Lower Valley Road
Atglen, PA 19310
Phone: (610) 593-1777; Fax: (610) 593-2002
E-mail: Info@schifferbooks.com
www.schifferbooks.com

Acknowledgments

As with all of my projects, this book would not have been possible without the generous help of many friends. Instrumental to the completion of this book were Pat Stansell, Massimo Foti, Thomas Anderson, Scott Taylor, Gordon Blaker, the staff at the US Army Artillery Museum, the staff and volunteers at the Patton Museum, and the staff at the National Archives. All photos not otherwise credited are from the Bundesarchiv. Most importantly, I am blessed to have the help and support of my wife, Denise, for which I am eternally grateful.

Contents

Introduction

Since its inception, artillery has been towed. Methods of self-propulsion began in World War I with the same motorized platforms that served as the basis for tanks. However, the automotive limits of these platforms forced the development toward separate towing vehicles such as tractors. The Germans began refining this concept in the early 1930s with the development of their line of half-track prime movers. These were quite successful in their intended role, although towed artillery cannot be brought into battery immediately upon arrival on the battlefield. Considerable preparation is necessary to unlimber the gun and move it into final position. Much of this work must be done by hand.

As far back as 1934, the German war planners envisioned production of self-propelled artillery weapons, both field artillery and antitank artillery. However, the initial vehicles of this type to be fielded were far from ideal. Rather than being purpose built, these early vehicles were adaptations. As their tank fleet aged and newer, heavier designs were produced, older components were freed up to be used in the production of self-propelled artillery vehicles to provide the Panzer and Panzergrenadier divisions with artillery support on an armored, fully tracked chassis. Components of the Panzer II were chosen to equip the Wespe 10.5 cm self-propelled gun, and a heaver platform based on components of the Panzer III and IV was chosen to mount the heavier 15 cm s.FH 18/1 L/3D howitzer.

Among the earliest of Germany's self-propelled field artillery was this vehicle, with a name almost as unwieldy as the vehicle itself—15 cm sIG 33 (Sf) auf Panzerkampfwagen I Ausf B. Like most of Germany's early attempts at self-propelled artillery, the vehicle was an adaptation of an obsolete tank chassis—in this case, a Panzerkampfwagen I Ausf. B. *National Archives*

As with the early self-propelled field artillery, Germany's early self-propelled antitank artillery was based on the obsolete Panzerkampfwagen I Ausf. B chassis. The vehicle was created by marrying the well-regarded Skoda 47 mm kanon PU.V vz. 36 gun to the obsolete tank chassis, creating the Panzerjäger I. *Patton Museum*

CHAPTER 1

Hummel

The Sd.Kfz.165 Hummel ("bumblebee") self-propelled, armored, 15 cm field howitzer, mounted on the hybrid Pz.Kpfw. III/IV chassis, was selected for what German army ordnance meant to be merely an interim solution until a chassis designed specifically as a self-propelled gun platform could be produced (as was the Wespe).

The 15 cm s.F.H. (heavy field howitzer) 18/1 was mounted on a specially designed Alkett/Rheinmetall-Borsig lengthened tank chassis known as the Geschützwagen III/IV. Components were adopted from the Panzer III and Panzer IV series of tanks. The Panzer III Ausf. J provided its final drive wheels and steering units along with its Zahnradfabrik SSG 77 transmission gearbox. The heavier Panzer IV was the source for the Maybach HL 120 TRM engine and cooling system. The suspension, idler, and track tension adjustment mechanism were also sourced from the Panzer IV. Only the hull and superstructure were newly designed for the interim vehicle.

After the prototype had been accepted and the vehicle went into series production, much of the assembly was shifted to other companies. Rheinmetall-Borsig/Alkett designed the Hummel, but assembly and manufacture were also accomplished by Deutsche Eisenwerke in Duisburg, which supplied all special fittings, while the company Deutsche Rohrmühlen, Muelheim/Ruhr took over production of armoring.

Sometime, apparently in 1944, the hull design was changed slightly, with the number of return rollers being reduced and the driver's compartment being enlarged to span nearly the full width of the vehicle.

Production of the vehicle, designated 15 cm sPz H 18/1 auf Fgst Pz III/IV (Sf) (Sd Kfz 165), began in February 1943 and continued for the duration of the war.

Ultimately, a total of 884 of the vehicles were reported to have been produced. Given the name "Hummel," the vehicles were deployed in batteries of six, with their first combat being July 5, 1943, while taking part in Operation Zitadelle.

Although built on what was essentially a medium tank chassis, the Hummel, at 24 tons, was thinly armored, especially the very high walls around the fighting compartment, necessitated by mounting the s.FH 18/1 above the engine. The armor was intended to provide protection against shell fragments and infantry rounds up to 7.92 mm.

Master tactician *General* Hermann Balck would have preferred that no such vehicles be used, since they were large targets that were difficult to conceal. Also, when the vehicle broke down, the gun, too, was put out of action—something that rarely happened with guns pulled by prime movers, which had nearly equal cross-country mobility.

Motorization ruled the day, since a considerable amount of German artillery was still horse drawn right thought the end of the war. Most modern postwar armies moved toward a predominance of self-propelled artillery, with a smaller percentage still moved via prime mover.

The Hummel was received by the troops with mixed reviews. The battalion composition of six Wespe and six Hummels was sound. The combination of 10.5 cm and 15 cm guns was suitable for a wide range of objectives during a division's attack or defense. The mechanization of artillery noticeably increased the speed of bringing the gun into position.

However, there were many complaints regarding the mobility. *General* Balck's premonition was largely proven to be true. In addition to badly trained drivers, the Panzer III/IV chassis was an antiquated automotive design that suffered from faulty running gear. Additionally, the main clutch and idlers often broke. In spite of the vehicle's weight of 24 tons, the suspension was overloaded. The lack of spare parts was never fully addressed.

There was one notable case in Italy when the artillerymen demanded their towed guns back. After three weeks of fighting, the battery of the 26th Panzer Division had only one Hummel left out of six. This was due to the mountainous terrain, which the Hummel was poorly suited to.

In overall design the foreign equivalent of the Hummel was slightly inferior. The US Gun Motor Carriage M12 had no fighting compartment at all, and the crew had to stand behind it while firing. The American vehicle was also slower and heavier and carried only ten rounds of ammunition. Mechanically, though, the M12 soared above the Hummel, with its more reliable radial engine and robust Lee/Sherman running gear.

Despite all these complaints, the self-propelled gun mount concept itself was proven correct and was finally fully realized with the introduction of the US M40 Gun Motor Carriage late in the war.

The prototype Hummel is seen here during trials. An elaborate muzzle brake has been proposed. This would have been extremely beneficial in keeping down dust stirred up by the muzzle blast of the weapon, and help conceal the deployed vehicles from counterbattery fire. However, its design was considered too complicated and expensive for series production. *Patton Museum*

The main assembly hall at Deutsche-Eisenwerke. Here the forward superstructures are being assembled, with larger rear-fighting-compartment components going together in the background.

With the lower hulls now fabricated, Panzer IV suspension components are being added. The presence of the drive sprockets indicates that the final drive assembly has already been installed.

With all the suspension components in place, the vehicles await the installation of the their armored upper superstructures. The interior bulkheads seen form the forward portion of the engine compartment.

All fighting-compartment armor is in place on these vehicles, and the guns have been installed. As prescribed by regulation, the guns have been delivered already painted in dark yellow, while the vehicles remain in their dark-red primer undercoating. *Thomas Anderson collection*

In the foreground, finished guns await delivery, while in the rear, units left in red primer await their final automotive testing. Only after this was finished would they be completely painted in overall dark yellow. *Thomas Anderson collection*

A newly finished Hummel undergoes testing. When not in use, the Hummel's 15 cm howitzer was locked in place by a large A-frame travel lock that was installed on the front of the hull. This prevented damage to the trunnions when the vehicle was moving across rough terrain. *Thomas Anderson collection*

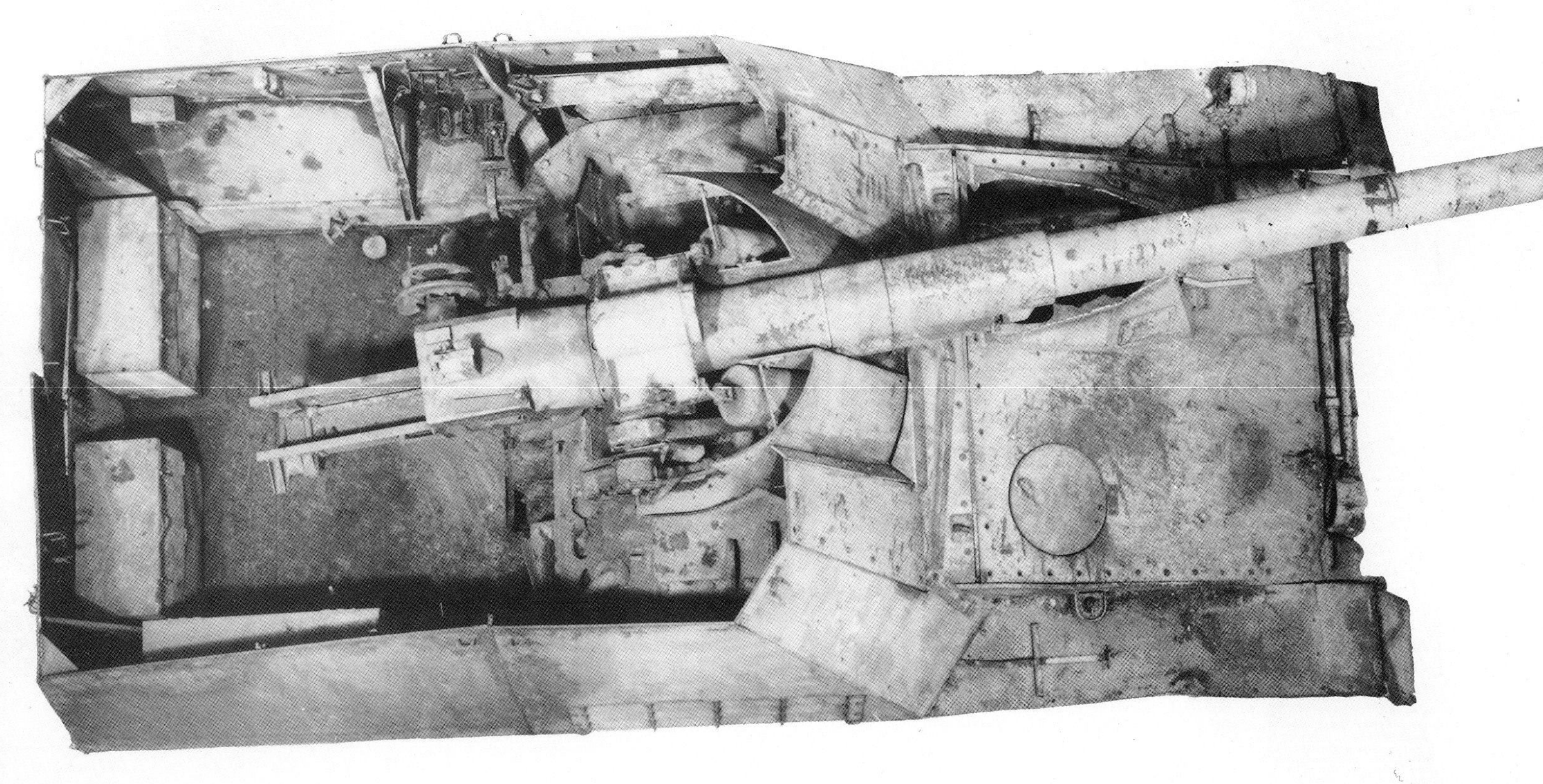

This overhead shot of a captured Hummel provides a good perspective of the overall layout of the vehicle. Limited traverse was possible, and large curved shields protected the gun mount and overlapped with the side armor. Eighteen projectiles could be carried in the bins at the rear, with eighteen charges stowed in the longer bin on the right side of the fighting compartment. *Patton Museum*

A brand new Hummel moves toward its firing position in the summer of 1943. Early-production vehicles can be immediately recognized by the two Bosch headlamps on either front fender. The large travel lock is still engaged here.

Having been directed to stop by the battery commander, the gun is now raised in preparation for firing. The first five Hummels were built in February 1943. In March, production reached twenty-six units, and forty-nine in April. Starting in May, the *Geschützwagen III für Munition* entered production, which decreased the number of Hummels being built. In total, 368 Hummels and ninety-six munitions carriers were built in 1943.

Again, directed by the battery commander, this gun is moving farther down the slope in order to maximize the cover of the terrain. Only limited movement was recommend with the travel lock disengaged. Heavy self-propelled gun batteries began to be formed in May 1943. According to TO&E K.St.N.461b, dated January 15, 1943, an *Abteilung* (battalion) comprised three batteries, two with Wespes and the third with the Hummel (Geschützwagen III/IV). The table also included two of the Hummel munitions carriers. A panzer artillery regiment of the Heer Panzer Division had three battalions.

Another brand-new Hummel battery traverses the summer steppe. All have travel locks and muzzle covers in place. The radio operator of the lead vehicle is carefully gauging the distance between vehicles, as indicated by regulation. The second and third vehicles have a large section of metal bar attached to the superstructure sides. This was used to store additional sections of spare track. This feature is also seen on some Nashorn self-propelled guns (SPGs).

The extremely new condition of these vehicles indicates that they may have just come from the railhead. There is little or no accumulation of dirt and mud anywhere on the suspension. The shipping stencil of the lead vehicle can be seen just behind the jack on the front left side of the superstructure. A small section of camouflage netting is stowed just behind the driver's head. *Patton Museum*

Two of the guns seen previously are now in position. Travel locks have been removed, sights have been installed, and the crews are awaiting orders. At this point, significant amounts of ammunition will be positioned in the rear of the vehicles in order to sustain the fire mission.

In order to disengage the substantial travel lock, it first had to be unclasped from the barrel. Then the two sections of the frame were detached and lowered to the front hull. For longer journeys, a locking mechanism located on the bottom of the breech slide was also used.

This and the following three photos show an SS unit as it prepares a firing position during the battle of Kursk. Shot through the driver's port, this view depicts the group dispersing into its firing position. Camouflage netting has been wrapped around the barrels in order to disguise the nature of these new weapons. A Wespe is visible in the background. *National Archives*

These Hummels are thought to belong to one of the three regiments of the 1st SS Panzergrenadier Division *Leibstandarte SS Adolf Hitler*. SS units were more lavishly equipped with the Hummel, sometimes having up to six or seven per battery. Travel locks have been disengaged here, and the camouflage material is being neatly stowed for future use. *National Archives*

The gun crew is waiting for the arrival of its ammunition train. A sustained fire mission would quickly exhaust the Hummel's onboard supply of shells and charges; only eighteen of each were carried. Typically, stacks of both were created in close proximity to each gun, where they could be quickly passed to the gun crew. *National Archives*

This battery of an army unit awaits the order to commence firing during the summer 1943 battles around Kursk. Crates of rounds and charges can be seen in the middle. Sheaves of long grass have been fastened to the superstructures in order to help conceal the guns on the open steppe. The vehicle to the left has a swastika flag on the top of the gun. This was a common and unmistakable aid in determining friend from foe.

Hummels of 3./Pz.A.R. *Großdeutschland* move into position. The very high silhouette of the vehicle, a shortcoming in any military vehicle, is evident. The ventilation flaps serve the centrally located HL 120 TRM engine. *GD* had a full six-gun battery by the start of Operation Zitadelle in July 1943, together with two of the complementary *Munitionsfahrzeuge* (ammunition carriers) Hummels, with the 15 cm gun removed to carry spare rounds. *Patton Museum*

Another shot of the 3./Pz.A.R. *Großdeutschland* guns on the move. The driver can be plainly seen through his vision aperture. Local foliage was also helpful in concealing the guns once in position. Like all Hummels, this one has a large section of spare track links mounted on a metal bar on the lower front hull. Spare parts were a constant issue with Hummel units. *Patton Museum*

A complete tarpaulin was stowed within the driver's compartment, but it was installed and used only on sustained road marches. Small loops were welded around the periphery of the firing compartment, which corresponded to leather straps on the tarp. The twin Bosch headlamps indicate an early-production vehicle.

Another group of Hummels on a long road march. The tactical insignia of the forwardmost vehicle indicates that these Hummels are guns of the Panzer-Artillerie-Regiment 116, which was the organic artillery unit of the 5th Panzer Division. This vehicle also mounts a removable step to aid the crew in mounting the vehicle. This is not a feature usually associated with the Hummel.

This well-camouflaged Hummel has received a thorough overspray of what are probably dark-green bands, although reddish brown was also prescribed in addition to the green. Local branches enhance the overall effect. The crewman riding on the fender appears to have his hand on a large wooden beam—an aid, perhaps, to the likelihood of encountering soft ground on its journey.

A somewhat rare view of the *Munitionsfahrzeuge* (ammunition carrier) Hummel. This was essentially a Hummel with the 15 cm gun removed to carry spare rounds. A metal plate was installed over the opening left by the removal of the gun. The *Munitionsfahrzeuge* carried thirty-four additional rounds, as opposed to the eighteen rounds carried on the Hummel itself. The *Munitionsfahrzeuge* could be quickly converted back to a standard Hummel if the need arose. *Patton Museum*

This and the next four photos depict an army unit undergoing familiarization training with its early Hummels in the fall of 1943. The nearest vehicle has a weather cover installed over the air intake on the left side. This is rarely seen on vehicles in the field. The crewman is beginning the task of removing the tight-fitting canvas muzzle cover.

This crewman is disengaging and lowering the travel lock. At his feet, a jack block can be seen within the coil of wire rope that forms the tow cable. To the left of center in the photo is the armored antenna mount. All Hummels were equipped with a Fu.Spr.Ger. f midband, high-frequency AM voice transceiver radio with a transmit power of 5 watts for interunit communication. This could be used either with a 1.4- or 2.0-meter antenna. It had a range of 5 kilometers. *Patton Museum*

The crews are now being instructed on the finer points of elevating the main weapon. Given that artillery units did not initially have tank parts within their logistics tail, having an ample supply of spare parts was an ongoing necessity for Hummel units. To this end, large brackets have been welded to the front of the superstructure, each mounting a complete road wheel assembly.

The unit workshops have also provided an interlaced array of steel wire on the superstructure sides, so that the crew can place locally culled branches while in their firing position. Interestingly, this vehicle mounts idler wheels more typically associated with the Panzer IV Ausf. D. Early vehicles such as this also mounted rubber-rimmed return rollers. *Patton Museum*

Here, a significant identifying feature of initial-production Hummels is illustrated: the early-pattern muffler. A long exhaust pipe emanated from each side of the engine compartment and culminated in a standard Panzer IV muffler housing. A metal rod was formed into steps on either side of the housing. This became highly unpopular with the crews, since it allowed exhaust into the fighting compartment and could overheat the ammunition charges stowed just above and inside the muffler mount. *Patton Museum*

A crewman manipulates the RblF 36 panoramic telescope gunsight. This was installed only once the gun had reached its firing position. This critical instrument was vital to the successful operation of the gun, and great care was taken not to damage it. Details of the under-superstructure tie-down are visible here.

The same crewman familiarizes himself with the elevation mechanism. It was important for all members of the crew to be knowledgeable about all aspects of the gun's operation. Various details of the breechblock, its actuating lever, the recuperator housing, and the trunnions all are visible here.

This Russian front Hummel of the 9th SS Division *Hohenstaufen* is wearing a carefully applied camouflage scheme of dark green over dark grey, a scheme that was not supposed to be used after spring 1943. Draped over the barrel is a camouflage net, with the supporting poles stowed on the travel lock. *Patton Museum*

This shot provides a better view of the elaborate antigrenade screen over the crew compartment. The Hummel's designers generally frowned on this type of modification, since it encouraged the use of the weapon at close quarters—something it was not designed to do. The thin armor combined with significantly vulnerable internal ammunition stowage made it poorly suited for the support role. *Patton Museum*

This close-up of another Hohenstaufen Hummel crew provides a good perspective of the uniform worn by its crew. They are dressed according to regulations regarding the crews of self-propelled guns, rather than as artillerymen, as in army units. Another spare road wheel has been installed on the front glacis plate. Additional wheels have probably been mounted on the rear superstructure as well.

A more sensible arrangement for the rear exhaust entered production in the summer of 1943. The separate pipes now terminated before the rear hull plate, and the ends were canted outward to direct gases away from the crew. The coiled hose seen within the firing compartment was used to transfer warm coolant from one vehicle to another—a valuable tool in cool weather.

This and the next several photographs depict a battery of Hummels, probably of Pz.A.R. *Großdeutschland*, as they begin assembly for a fire mission in the winter of 1943–44. Here, the unit has overtaken a line of Sturmgeschütze assault guns. All Hummel batteries consisted of six guns, rather than the four contained in a towed battery, since two of the SPGs were usually unavailable for various mechanical reasons. *Patton Museum*

This vehicle has presented its profile to the camera as it executes a turn in front of the line of Sturmgeschütze. Given its size and logistical priority, *Großdeutschland*'s unit workshops were always busy providing useful modifications and enhancements. Large storage boxes are installed on one or both fenders in this battery, helping alleviate the lack of stowage space within the vehicle. In this instance the jack as been relocated slightly forward of its original position. *Patton Museum*

The same Hummel is seen farther along its journey. The driver's compartment is fully buttoned up here, with its large visor sealed against the front of the cabin. The Hummel's normal crew consisted of a driver, a radioman, and four gunners for the 15 cm s.FH 18/1 L/30. An MG 34 or 42 mounted on the fighting compartment provided modest antiaircraft protection but is not often seen installed. *Patton Museum*

Elements of the battery pause in front of a small group of structures, while other vehicles move farther forward. This battery appears to have at least five guns, or possibly more. The forwardmost Hummel has two stowage boxes installed on the front fenders.

The battery has paused to review their final orders and firing dispositions. Many of the crewmen are making good use of their pattern 1943 reversible camouflage parkas. It is interesting to see that many of the vehicles shown in this series are marked with a chassis number stenciled on the hull. Hummel production received the serial numbers 320001–32813. *Patton Museum*

As directed by the battalion commander, these two guns will take up a firing position among the buildings. Identified by their chassis numbers, these are 320262 and 320264. The radio operator of the left-hand vehicle is in front, directing the gun back into position. Gun travel locks will remain in place until movement is complete. *Patton Museum*

Hummel 320264 moves into position atop a small rise in the terrain. Although it does not appear to be its final stop, such a feature could provide additional elevation for the main gun. This was not usually a problem for the 15 cm s.FH 18/1, since its range was an impressive 14,630 yards. *Patton Museum*

The crew has wrapped themselves up well for the cold. The frame device ahead of the driver's position of this and many other Hummels was designed as an aid in roughly aiming the gun, in conjunction with preplaced aiming stakes. Details of the spare track and its attachment points are also visible here. *Patton Museum*

The crew of gun 320264 continues its preparation for firing. The gun travel lock has been lowered and the interior tarpaulins are being stowed. The large hook seen in the center of the photo was used to allow a single soldier to install the travel lock, by pulling one section up with the hook while raising the other from the same position.

Another good close-up of 320264 reveals details of the driver's cabin, with its visors, hatch, and front viewing aperture. The driver's and radio operator's hatches were identical. Like the crews of other German armored vehicles, the Hummel's was issued with headphones and interphones for internal communication.

Details of the driver's front viewing aperture are clearly seen here. All portions of the assembly were painted in the vehicle's exterior color (in this case, dark yellow) except the glass block section, which was painted in the standard German military vehicle interior color of off-white.

Hummels 320262 and 320264 are now seen astride a small windmill. It is likely that these shots are providing material for a training manual, illustrating the best methods for exploiting terrain when selecting and creating efficient firing positions. Such a concealed position could be useful in avoiding counterbattery fire.

Yet another gun has taken its concealment to the extreme. It has burrowed into a small depression in between two buildings, and its crew is proceeding to cover it with sheaves of tall cut grasses. Such a position would be very difficult to detect, even from the air. Conversely, such a position could take time to evacuate in the event that it was discovered.

The battery has now proceeded to a more opening position. Given the elevation of the forwardmost guns, this time it appears that firing will soon commence. The large rear doors of the firing compartments are laid wide open to facilitate the movement of rounds and charges, which will soon arrive to be stacked behind the guns.

Close examination of this photo reveals that the two vehicles in the foreground are Hummels 320262 and 320264, seen previously in this series. The Sturmgeschütz unit depicted in the first shot of this sequence has now overtaken the battery and may be moving to support the infantry attack that the firing mission will be assisting.

This Hummel crew has added several vertical branches to help disguise their mount—a seemingly futile gesture in this bleak, open winter position. In the background to the right, several wicker containers can be seen; these were cushioned containers for the 15 cm rounds.

A well-whitewashed Hummel also is the beneficiary of local foliage. This gun has the substantial added advantage of actually being emplaced within the same living trees. The white winter paint has been applied over the entire superstructure of the firing compartment, except for a small square around the national insignia.

A mixed group of Hummels and Wespes proceed through a Russian town. This Hummel is loaded with extra provisions and crew gear. The presence of a fuel drum on the front deck is an unusual but practical solution for providing spare fuel on a long road march. Other photos in this series indicate that this vehicle is towing a small trailer. *Patton Museum*

A major advantage of the Hummel is that it required no special preparation for rail travel. Whole units could be entrained rapidly. The markings on these cars are in German, indicating travel within western Europe. This is a full unit of self-propelled guns, as evidenced by the presence of a Wespe SPG on the extreme left. *Patton Museum*

An especially advantageous firing position is one that could be disguised from enemy artillery by a natural terrain feature. Here, a battery is located behind a large hill during the winter of 1944. This position has been sustained for some time, as evidenced by the considerable amount of ammunition-packing material and the general deterioration of the snow.

This shot provides a closer view of one of the battery's vehicles. The large tarpaulin for the firing compartment can be seen pushed over the left side of the superstructure. A spare crate has been placed behind the rear hull to use as a step while passing rounds to the gun crew. The generally worn state of the winter camouflage is of interest.

In this third view of the winter battery in action, we see the large number of shells stacked along the rear edge of the opening in the superstructure. It would be at this point that the fuses would be added to the shells. A full fourteen shells have been unpacked and stand on the two packing cases in the foreground.

As a precaution, the shells were always kept some distance from the gun until they were ready to be fired. At that point they were ferried to the crew as they were needed. Four members of the battery are accomplishing this task—no small feat, since the shells weighed nearly 100 pounds each.

A battery of four Hummels engage in a sustained-fire mission in the early spring of 1944. The Panzer IV/III drive sprocket of the vehicle usually had an unarmored hub installed on its center. This was used to protect the many lug nuts from moisture damage. Accidents or combat could shear them away, although they were required to be reinstalled when practicable.

This rather dramatic shot was probably a contrivance of the cameraman rather than a genuine night shot. Due to rapid counterbattery fire, sustained use of artillery at night was not considered prudent, unless in the case of a surprise attack or an emergency.

A common field modification was the addition of a wooden structure for the opening of the firing compartment. With this in place, crewmen could align several rounds where the gun crew could quickly grab them. A variety of ammunition-packing containers and materials litter the background.

This early-model Hummel is part of the collection of the Panzer Museum in Münsterlager, home of the modern German army's tank-training center. It is fully restored and is a runner. The gun still fires, and it is frequently used for demonstration purposes. *Massimo Foti*

A large, modern-style camouflage net is stowed on top of the vehicle. This vehicle has the late-style, all-metal return rollers and spare road wheels stored on the rear hull. *Massimo Foti*

The various details of the driver's cabin are seen here. Later vehicles had an enlarged cabin that spanned the full width of the front end. *Massimo Foti*

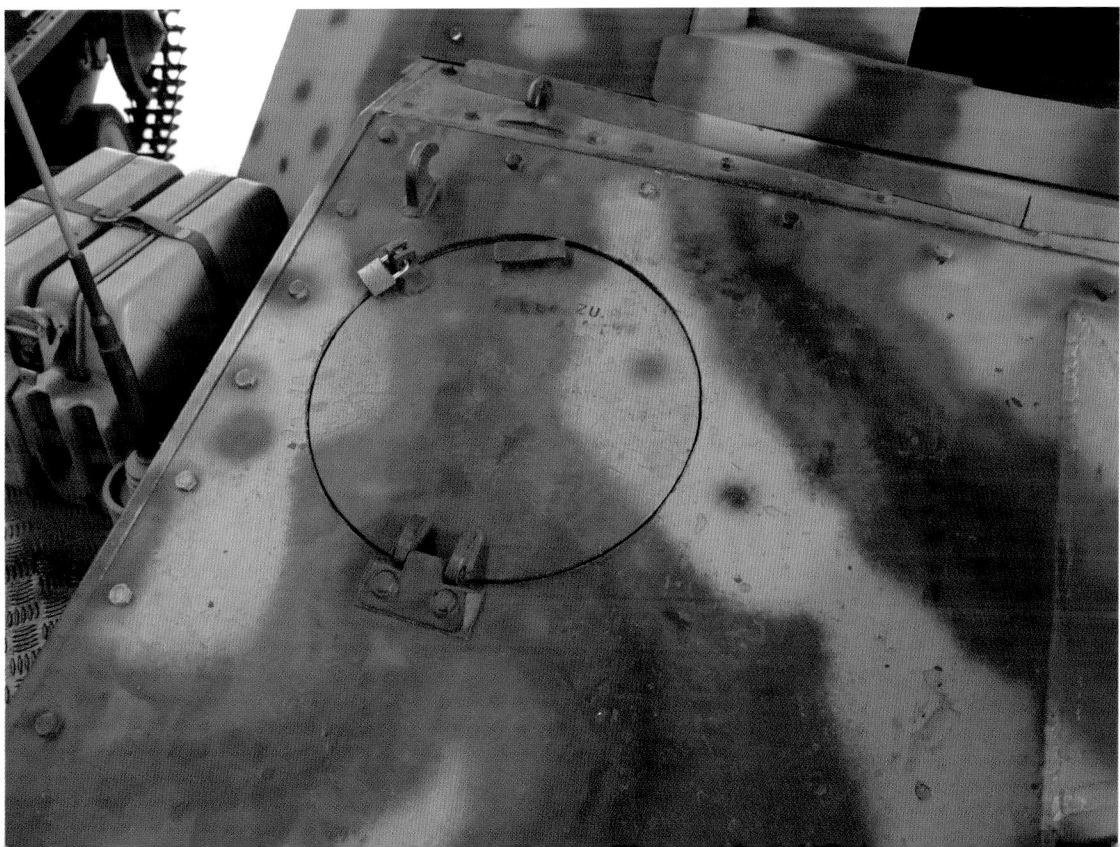

A close-up of the circular hatch on top of the radio operator's position. Compared to that of the driver, this position was quite cramped. *Massimo Foti*

The vehicle's jack is of a slightly more modern type. The tread plate that makes up the surface of the front fenders is also a modern material. *Massimo Foti*

Hummel Specifications

Length	7.17 m
Width	2.97 m
Height	2.81 m
Weight	23 tons
Fuel capacity	600 liters
Maximum speed	25 km/hr.
Range, on road	215 km
Range, cross-country	135 km
Crew	6
Communications	Fu.Spr.Ger. f
Weapon, main	15 cm s.F.H. 18/1
Weapon, secondary	MG 34
Ammo stowage, main	18 rounds
Ammo stowage, secondary	600 rounds
Range	13,250 meters

Armor, chassis	30 mm front 20 mm sides and rear carbon steel
Armor, superstructure	10 mm
Engine make	Maybach
Engine model	HL 120 TRM
Engine configuration	V-12, liquid cooled
Engine displacement	11.9 liters
Engine horsepower	265 @2,600 rpm

A later-model Hummel can be found at the French armor museum in Saumur. It has the full-width crew cabin introduced in February 1944. *Massimo Foti*

The Saumur Hummel was knocked out by a hit to the left side of the driver's cabin. Additional damage was also sustained on the left drive sprocket. *Massimo Foti*

A close-up of the left towing lug. This area was generally reinforced with extra steel plate to prevent the loop from shearing way when the vehicle was towed. *Massimo Foti*

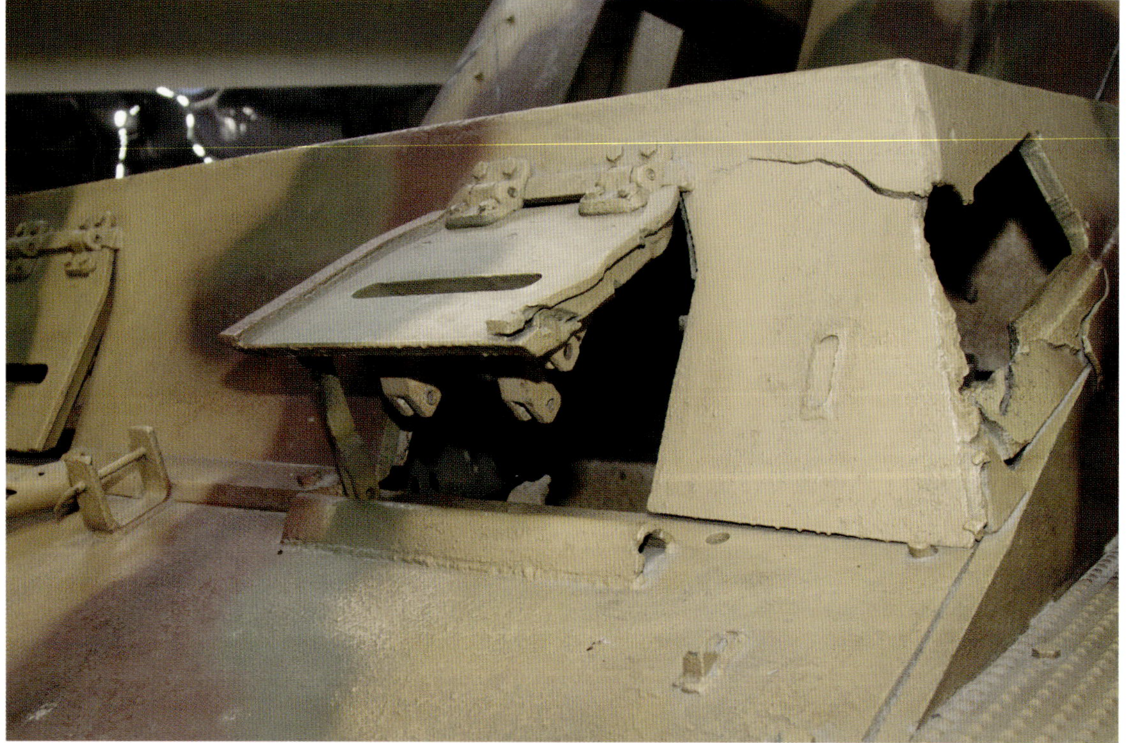

The front driver's aperture of the Saumur was damaged by the shell hit. The impact removed the left-hand door brace as well. *Massimo Foti*

Details of the left-hand hinge base of the travel lock are seen here, as are the hoods for the brake-cooling openings. *Massimo Foti*

Details of the right-hand base of the travel lock are evident, as are details of the lock itself. One of the lock legs had been heavily pierced with shrapnel. *Massimo Foti*

The radio operator's vision aperture, which is identical to that of the driver. Details of the tow cable lock are visible at the right. *Massimo Foti*

A single suspension unit of the Münsterlager vehicle. Each was suspended with multiple leaf springs. *Massimo Foti*

A close-up view of one of the eight all-metal return rollers. *Massimo Foti*

The large rear doors that permitted access to the firing compartment. *Massimo Foti*

This large slotted and armored ventilation panel was one of two on the Hummel and corresponded to the location of the engine just beneath it. *David Doyle*

The idler wheel was of tubular construction and could also be found on the Panzer IV F through H. *David Doyle*

Metal rod was formed into brackets that firmly engaged the gap between the two pairs of road wheels. Two of these brackets were found on the lower rear hull. *David Doyle*

One of the two long exhaust pipe assemblies found underneath the superstructure on each side of the Hummel. *David Doyle*

The Panzer III/IV–style drive sprocket of the Saumur vehicle is missing its protective hub cover. The damage to the sprocket is evident here as well. *Massimo Foti*

Details of the bracket that attached the exhaust pipe assembly to the hull. *Massimo Foti*

The point at which the exhaust pipe exited the hull had an armored cover and two additional brackets. *Massimo Foti*

This small plate was meant to push loose track pins back into place as they passed over it. *Massimo Foti*

This shot reveals details of the rear towing hook, the spare wheels, the rear step, and the brackets for the stowage of the aiming stakes. *Massimo Foti*

The right-side rear towing hook, muffler, spare wheel, and track pin plate. *Massimo Foti*

The bottom of the firing compartment was not armored and could be found pierced by fasteners that secured boxes and brackets inside. *Massimo Foti*

This box, located at the right rear of the firing compartment, could hold fifteen charges in secured holders. Its cover is missing on this example. *Massimo Foti*

An overall view of the firing compartment as seen from the rear. In spite of some missing equipment, it is largely intact. *Massimo Foti*

Details of the breech and interior structure can be seen here, as can the charge stowage box on the right. The bracket at the upper left is for stowing the coolant transfer hose. *Massimo Foti*

This pipe could be regulated with a small door to allow warm air from the engine into the firing compartment during cold weather. *Massimo Foti*

A view from the rear doors, looking down at the access panels that covered the fuel tanks. The fuel filler necks can be seen at the far left. *Massimo Foti*

Various bracket and attachment points are visible here on the left side of the superstructure. Stowage for the gunsight was in the large box seen at the right side of the photo. Its lid is missing. *Massimo Foti*

A closer view of one of two large brackets that braced the sides of the superstructure. Just below it, a portion of the internal gun travel lock can be seen. *Massimo Foti*

CHAPTER 2

Nashorn/Hornisse

Germany entered World War II with the 3.7 cm PaK 36 as its standard antitank gun. One of this gun's primary advantages was that its small crew could easily handle it. Leather harnesses were even provided for the crewmen to facilitate towing it across short distances. Experience with the heavier French tanks in 1940 spurred on the development of heavier antitank guns. First the 5 cm gun and then the even heavier 7.5 cm gun were introduced. The 5 cm gun was provided with an extra wheel, but still it took a crew of five to move it into position. The 7.5 cm gun weighed over a ton, and its crew of eight endured considerable effort to move it around the battlefield.

The increasing need to deal with the more heavily armed Russian tanks finally led to the development of the 8.8 cm PaK 43. Developed by Krupp, the 8.8 cm PaK 43/41 (the PaK designated tank cannon—*panzer kanone*, versus FlaK, or *Flugzeugabwehrkanone*—aircraft-defense cannon) had a 71-caliber barrel (heavy gun calibers are determined by dividing the length of the barrel by the bore) and fired a round with an 822 mm long cartridge case.

Designed as a towed antitank weapon, its weight and bulk presented significant challenges. In order to get it to the front faster and in greater numbers, it was decided to find a self-propelled mount for it.

It was quickly determined that a ready-made mount was already in existence in the form of the Geschützwagen für sFH 18/1, which had recently entered production for the Hummel self-propelled artillery piece. The dual use of the chassis was especially pleasing to Hitler.

On January 22, 1943, Altmärkische Kettenwerke GmbH (Alkett) in Dusseldorf signed a contract for 420 Hornisse. The factory was to reach its full rate of production of thirty vehicles per month in March. An additional contract for 150 Hornisse was signed with Deutsche Eisenwerke AG, Werk Stahlindustie, on the same day. The first five vehicles were planned for May 1943, and fifteen per month were planned from July 1943 to March 1944. The total production of the Hornisse was planned to be 570 vehicles. However, ultimately Alkett produced 370 of the vehicles, and Deutsche-Eisenwerke AG completed 124 at their facility in Teplitz-Schönau. Alkett stopped building the Hornisse in May 1944.

Note on Terminology

This gun was frequently referred to as the *Hornisse* (hornet). The term "8.8 cm Panzerjäger 43/1 (L/71) Hornisse" was also used in the manual. Hornisse was perhaps the most popular among the troops.

However, on June 6, 1944, the 6th Department of the Armament Directorate, as previously directed by Hitler, began using the name *Nashorn* (rhinoceros) to refer to these vehicles. The name had been used previously, but now it was official. However, some documents still referred to it as Hornisse.

Only fourteen vehicles were delivered in February 1944. Hummel production was to be of the highest priority, given their inclusion in tank division artillery batteries, while the Hornisse was of lower priority. Deutsche Eisenwerke did not end up building a single Hornisse, switching entirely to Hummels. Although Alkett remained the sole production source, rates of production were high: thirty in March, forty-one in April, and thirty-five both in May and June. As a result of this, field units started to be formed in late March.

Production was kept up through the summer and fall, with eighty vehicles made, but a significant British bombing raid forced the relocation of the facilities, and the total number manufactured in 1943 was 345. The last twenty-five vehicles were delivered in February 1944. Alkett ended up building 370 in total, with chassis serial numbers 310001–310370.

Production of the Hornisse may well have ended without the attendant difficulties. It had not been well received at the front. In spite of the excellent performance of the gun, the same automotive difficulties that plagued the Hummel were also besetting the Hornisse—exacerbated by its additional 2 tons of weight. Additionally, the vehicles had virtually no armor protection.

The fully armored and enclosed Jagdpanther was conceived as the replacement for the Hornisse, but demand for the Panther chassis meant that production would have to continue temporarily if the troops were to have any type of heavy self-propelled antitank gun at all.

As a result, Hornisse production was moved to Werk Teplitz-Schönau in the Czech city of Teplice. Production began in April, when twenty vehicles were delivered. One hundred were to be built in Teplice by June 1944. It was hoped that production of the Jagdpanther would soon begin in earnest, since the army still had a significant need for these resources to build Hummels. However, Werk Teplitz-Schönau built only 108 vehicles in 1944.

Another small run of Nashorns was made in January 1945, with sixteen vehicles built before March, when production at Werk Teplitz-Schönau ended. In total, 124 Nashorns with serial numbers 310371–310500 were built there.

In the end, the overall design was quite flawed. Although the performance of the gun was considered excellent, the best performance was found to be at very long ranges, where the threat of counterattack was sparse. Because of its 30 mm armor, any type of close engagement spelled doom for the crews. At nearly 3 meters in height, it was not easily hidden on the battlefield. The vehicle's occasional use as an assault gun was even more disastrous.

Like the Hummel it was based on, it was the severe automotive shortcomings of the chassis that finally did in the Nashorn. For instance, in August 31, 1943, the s.Pz.Jg.Abt 560 could count on only eighteen vehicles ready for combat out of a total of thirty-one. The s.Pz.Jg.Abt 655 had forty Hornisse, with only twenty-six of them functional. By December 30, 1944, just 165 Hornisse were left of 478 produced, with only 130 still fit for combat.

The Hornisses were gradually replaced with Jagdpanther and Jagdpanzer IV tank destroyers, but as in the US Army, the basic premise of a tank destroyer arm was found to be deficient. A good antitank platform was never going to be a substitute for a good tank.

This Nashorn, very early production, has the conventional muffler arrangement, although a short section of pipe has been added to the top of this muffler to direct gases away from the crew compartment. Another feature of very early vehicles is seen here: the Panzer III E–style drive sprocket. Interestingly, this is not seen on the Hummel. This is no doubt due to its production by Alkett, which was also engaged in the production of the Panzer III–based Sturmgeschütze.

Another early-production Nashorn moves along a road in Italy in 1944. In order to disguise it from the air, it has been heavily covered in foliage. Unlike the Hummel, Nashorn crews tended to install their tow cables either on the front hull or the rear hull, rather than coiled on top.

Having all the ammunition stowed in unarmored containers, combined with the Nashorn's thin armor, often proved disastrous for the crew. This destroyed vehicle is being examined by troops from New Zealand. TO&E K.St.N 1148b, for a Hornisse, specified that a battery would consist of ten vehicles, six of which were split between three platoons; of the remaining four vehicles, three remained in reserve and one would be equipped both with FuG 8 and FuG 5 radios, to be used by the battery commander. *Patton Museum*

Due to the amount of ammunition carried, more often than not the destruction of Nashorns was complete. These ANZAC soldiers are looking for souvenirs among the shattered remains of this 1./525 s. Pz.Jg.Abt vehicle near Cassino. This battalion had been formed in the spring of 1943 along with the s.Pz. Jg.Abt 655. The 560th and 655th battalions reached battle readiness in May 1943. In July 1943, they first saw action during Operation Zitadelle. *Patton Museum*

The later Nashorn had the spare road wheel racks located on the rear of the vehicle, and the barrel-style muffler of the early vehicles was eliminated. These entrained vehicles all have their foul-weather tarps installed—an essential piece of equipment on the open-topped Nashorn. The bands of camouflage on the interior of the rear door are of interest. *Patton Museum*

Some interim vehicles were built with the early travel lock, but with the spare road wheels relocated to the rear. On March 25, 1943, three batteries were integrated into the 560th Heavy Tank Destroyer Battalion (s.Pz.Jg.Abt 560). On April 1, a variant of the K.St.N 1148b TO&E was approved, now with fourteen vehicles per battery. Now there were two commander's SPGs, and each platoon counted four Hornisse. *Patton Museum*

The canvas cover provided for the fighting compartment was primarily used in rear areas, or when in transit. It functioned chiefly to protect the weapon and ammunition. The rarely seen interior travel lock is in place here. It consisted of two large bars that engaged the gun slide and each interior wall. A similar mechanism was available for the Hummel. *Patton Museum*

The Nashorn was never fitted with the full-width driver's cabin developed for the late Hummel. Instead, the narrow, protruding compartment shown here was used throughout the war. A battalion, according to TO&E K.St.N. 1155b, approved on March 30, 1943, included three batteries plus three Hornisse in the HQ. A battalion of Hornisses had a total of forty-five tank destroyers. *Patton Museum*

Another Nashorn captured in Italy becomes the object of amusement for a group of British soldiers. This vehicle is equipped with the late-style remote-release type of barrel clamp. The tube for the cable runs alongside the driver's cabin. *Patton Museum*

When captured intact, Allied troops not only examined the powerful tank-killers but used them against their former owners. Originally known as the *Hornisse*, or "hornet," on January 27, 1944, Hitler ordered it renamed *Nashorn*, or "rhinoceros." *Patton Museum*

The Nashorn's 8.8 cm gun was well suited for antitank duty but was less than ideal as field artillery. Nevertheless, His Majesty's troops are using this captured vehicle for just that. The range of the gun was 17,500 meters, allowing it to fire from beyond the range of most other cannon. *Patton Museum*

A battery proceeds along a road in the winter of 1943–44. Two new Nashorn battalions had been formed in August–September 1943: the 93rd and 519th. In December 1943, they were joined by the s.Pz.Jg.Abt 88. It was the last to receive the nominal forty-five vehicles. In total, six battalions entirely equipped with the Hornisse were formed. Twelve more were received by the 664th Tank Destroyer Battalion, which also had towed PaK 43 guns. *Patton Museum*

A Nashorn crew prepares dinner for the battery. This gun has a thorough camouflage paint scheme, which would help offset the disadvantage of the vehicle's thin armor. The rack on the very rear of the hull was used to stow the gun-cleaning rods. These crewmen have installed their towrope across the spare road wheels.

Like the Hummel, the fuel tanks of the Nashorn were found beneath the floor and behind the main gun. The fuel filler necks were located to the left of floor panels. Pumping fuel that distance using a hand-operated device could be quite difficult. This crew is employing log beams to lift a fuel drum into the fighting compartment in order to use gravity to assist in this difficult process.

The crew of a Nashorn nicknamed "Puma" bombs up in the winter of 1944. This crew has added a wire array across the large superstructure sides in order to attach foliage in the warmer months. Unpacking and loading the heavy rounds was an arduous task that took the efforts of the entire battery. *Patton Museum*

A close-up of the driver's cabin of "Puma" shows the general deterioration of the winter paint scheme. A spare road wheel has been installed next to the cabin, behind the jack. An elaborate unit insignia has become visible on the superstructure, rubbed clean of the winter whitewash.

An MG 34 machine gun and two MP 40 submachine guns were supplied with the Nashorn and were used to defend against enemy infantry. The chance of such action was much more likely with the Nashorn as compared to the Hummel, which was primarily used much farther from the front.

The crew of this Nashorn has added large wooden planks to the front hull. This may have been an attempt to increase the scant armor protection of the vehicle. Given its location on the top of the spare track links, it probably served that purpose well. This vehicle also has the V-shaped ice cleats installed on its tracks. *Patton Museum*

The extremely long barrel of the 88 required a travel lock during noncombat maneuvers. In this view the travel lock has been released. This was done by raising the barrel and allowing the dowel (seen extending under the barrel, directly above the drive sprocket in this view) to disengage the support. This was then lowered against the hull by springs. *Patton Museum*

Nashorn/Hornisse Specifications

Length	8.44 m
Width	2.95 m
Height	2.94 m
Weight	24 tons
Fuel capacity	600 liters
Maximum speed	40 km/hr.
Range, on road	260 km
Range, cross-country	130 km
Crew	5
Communications	Fu.Spr.Ger. f
Weapon, main	8.8 cm PaK43/1 L/71
Traverse: manual, ±15°	
Elevation: manual, +20/–5°	
Primary gunsight: Sfl. Z. F. 1a (Selbstfahrlafetten-Zielfernrohr)	
Magnification: 5×	
Field of view: 8°	
Indirect fire sight: Aushilfsrichtmittel 38	
Magnification: 3×	
Field of view: 10°	
Weapon, secondary	MG 34 or MG 42
Ammo stowage, main	40
Ammo stowage, secondary	600
Armor, superstructure sides and gun shield	10 mm
Glacis	15 mm
Hull front	30 mm
Hull side	20 mm
Engine make	Maybach
Engine model	HL 120 TRM
Engine configuration	V-12, liquid cooled
Engine displacement	11.9 liters
Engine horsepower	265 @2,600 rpm

The high silhouette of the Nashorn is evident in this winter scene. In April 1943, starting with vehicle number 51, a periscopic Sfl.ZF.1a gunsight was used instead of a telescopic ZF 3 × 8 gunsight. In May, the thickness of the gun shield was increased from 10 to 15 mm, and a half ring was added behind the mobile gun shield.

A good close-up of the driver's cabin. Like the Hummel, very early Nashorns had two Bosch headlamps, while later vehicles such as this had only one. The single-dot pattern of the standard World War II German tread plate is seen to good advantage here on the front fender. *Patton Museum*

The Nashorn was designed as a direct-fire weapon, intended to fire its projectile along a line of sight. The cannon's long range and the vehicle's mobility were its defense, since its thin armor and open top offered the crew little protection. Proper camouflage was critical, as in this hidden position between two structures. *Patton Museum*

The famed 88 unleashed. The Nashorn was capable of engaging targets at extreme ranges, much to the detriment of its opponents. The combination of the 8.8 cm PaK 43 gun and high-quality Zeiss optics was a lethal one.

This Nashorn crew is demonstrating for the camera the speed at which it can bring the gun into action. A spare radio antenna is mounted on the inside of the hull wall. A stowage container for the single-piece 8.8 cm rounds is located underneath. *Patton Museum*

Once the Nashorn was pulled into a firing position, the Sfl.ZF.la, RblF 36 3 × 8-degree monocular periscopic gunsight was passed to the gunner for installation. The breech still has its protective cover fitted at this time. *Patton Museum*

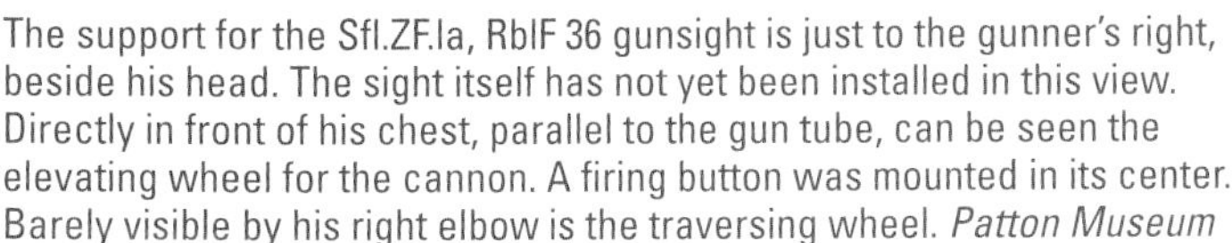

The support for the Sfl.ZF.Ia, RblF 36 gunsight is just to the gunner's right, beside his head. The sight itself has not yet been installed in this view. Directly in front of his chest, parallel to the gun tube, can be seen the elevating wheel for the cannon. A firing button was mounted in its center. Barely visible by his right elbow is the traversing wheel. *Patton Museum*

German optics were finely made pieces of equipment and were transported in padded cases and installed only immediately prior to firing. *Patton Museum*

Dispersing ammunition to guns in the battery usually fell to a single vehicle. The balance of the ammunition was typically stowed in shipping containers on the floor and in the rear of the fighting compartment. The scissors telescope has been installed. *Patton Museum*

A view of the same vehicle looking back from the front of the hull. This shot illustrates details of the gunner's position. *Patton Museum*

The ammunition was shipped in round metal tubes, which in turn were transported inside rectangular wooden boxes. *Patton Museum*

Today, only three Nashorns survive, one under restoration in private hands, one in the US Army collection, and this example displayed at the Patriot Museum, Kubinka, Russia. *Alan Wilson from Stilton, Peterborough, Cambridgeshire, UK*

The armored antenna base was installed just outside the radio operator's compartment. *Pat Stansell*

A close-up view of the jack block bracket. The jack block was typically a large, steel-reinforced block of wood. *Pat Stansell*

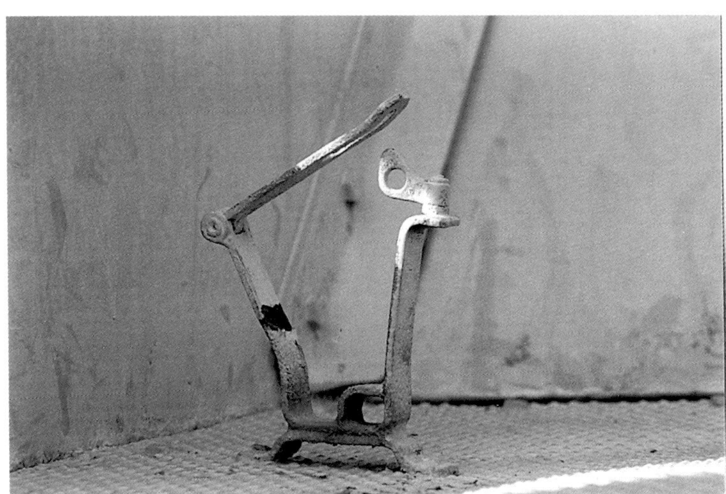

One of two substantial brackets used to secure the vehicle's jack. *Pat Stansell*

These heavy hinges allowed the driver's vision aperture to be raised for better visibility in noncombat situations. *Pat Stansell*

A detail view of the spring used to lower the travel lock. *Pat Stansell*

The Nashorn was provided with a MG 34 for close-in defense. Six hundred rounds of ammunition were carried for the machine gun, which mounted on this arm. *Pat Stansell*

This bracket once mounted the commander's scissor periscope. *Pat Stansell*

A detail shot of the locking mechanism that secured the rear fighting-compartment door. *Pat Stansell*

An interior view of the fighting compartment, left side, looking rearward. A portion of the internal wiring for the onboard intercom is still visible, as are the remains of one of the machine pistol stowage brackets. *Pat Stansell*